Saint
Alph
E   Day

OTHER BOOKS IN THE SERIES

Saint
Alphonsus Liguori
for
Every Day

Edited by
Trent Beattie

Paulist Press
New York/Mahwah, NJ

Cover image of Saint Alphonsus Liguori by Gaetano Domenichini, St. Paul's Church, Ferrara, Italy.
Cover design by Sharyn Banks
Book design by Lynn Else

Library of Congress Cataloging-in-Publication Data

Liguori, Alfonso Maria de', Saint, 1696–1787.
    [Selections. English. 2010]
    Saint Alphonsus Liguori for every day / edited by Trent Beattie.
        p. cm.
    Includes bibliographical references.
    ISBN 978-0-8091-4656-7 (alk. paper)
    1. Devotional calendars—Catholic Church. I. Beattie, Trent. II. Title.
BX2170.C56L54 2010
242'.2—dc22

                                                    2009041049

Published by Paulist Press
997 Macarthur Boulevard
Mahwah, New Jersey 07430

www.paulistpress.com

Printed and bound in the United States of America

Contents

This book is dedicated to the Holy Family:
Jesus, Mary, and Joseph

What breathtaking awe accompanies the thought
of God becoming man, of a creature becoming
the Mother of God, and of another creature
acting as the vicar of God the Father on earth!
Jesus Christ lived out the will of God
without peer, yet among mere creatures,
no one lived out the will of God
better than Mary and Joseph.

It is not necessary to be rich in this world, to gain the esteem of others, to lead a life of ease....It is only necessary to love God and to do His will. For this single end He created us, for this He preserves our life; and thus only can we gain admittance into Heaven.

—Saint Alphonsus Liguori

Introduction

Saint Alphonsus Liguori (1696–1787) earned a double doctorate in canon and civil law at the age of sixteen, founded the Congregation of the Most Holy Redeemer (more commonly known as the Redemptorists) at the age of thirty-six, became bishop of the Diocese of Saint Agatha of the Goths at the age of sixty-six, and was for many years a much-admired mission preacher and spiritual director. Had he not written a single word for publication, Saint Alphonsus still would have had quite an outstanding life, influencing thousands of souls for the better.

However, the great Italian saint *did* write for publication and in fact became the most published author in history. Over 21,500 editions of his works have been printed to date, in over 60 languages! This is an indication of the great influence he had within the Church on many topics, including Marian doctrine, the infallibility of the pope, and the necessity of prayer for salvation. He also made an outstanding contribution to moral theology. In 1987, Pope John Paul II said,

Alphonsus was responsible for the renewal of moral theology; through contact with the people he encountered in the confessional, especially during his missionary preaching, he gradually and with much hard work brought about a change in his mentality, progressively achieving a correct balance between rigorism and liberty. (Apostolic letter *Spiritus Domini*, marking the bicentenary of the death of Saint Alphonsus)

In the same document, the holy father said that Saint Alphonsus "had, as few others did, the *sensus Ecclesiae* [sense of the Church], a criterion that remained with him in his theological research and pastoral practice in such a way that he became, in a certain sense, the voice of the Church." Is it possible to receive higher praise than being called "the voice of the Church" by the Vicar of Christ?

This "voice of the Church" was put into writing in 111 different works, among the most popular of which are *Visits to the Blessed Sacrament, The Glories of Mary, The Practice of the Love of Jesus Christ, The Great Means of Salvation and of Perfection, Preparation for Death, Uniformity with God's Will,* and *The Way of the Cross.* While the works of Saint Alphonsus cover nearly every aspect of the Catholic faith, they can be summed up in one phrase: *the will of God*. As the saint said so well himself, "All perfection and sanctity consists in doing the Will of God," and, "The Divine Will is the rule of all goodness and virtue."

How is one to obtain the strength to do the will of God and to conform himself to it? In large part through prayer, which Saint Alphonsus taught to be morally necessary for salvation, saying bluntly that "he who prays is certainly saved; he who prays not is certainly damned." Prayer enabled Saint Alphonsus to get through his own intense sufferings of mind (most notably with scrupulosity) and of body (most notably with arthritis). The problems he faced in his own life contributed to the fact that his writings were concerned with real problems of real people, not with theoretical speculation.

Saint Alphonsus Liguori was canonized by Pope Gregory XVI in 1839, declared a doctor of the church in 1871 by Pope Pius IX, and named patron of confessors and moralists in 1950 by Pope Pius XII. Saint Alphonsus is a unique and illustrious saint whose insistence on the centrality of the will of God remains just as important today as it was in the 1700s.

*Saint Alphonsus Liguori, "voice of the Church,"
pray for us to have the light to know, and the
strength to do, the will of God in all things.*

[Editor's note: Liguori's traditional use of male pro-
nouns has been kept for the most part because chang-
ing so many references to "he or she" and "his or her"
would be more distracting than the original. However,
references to "man" or "men" are more noticeable and
thus have been changed and bracketed.]

January

Humility

1

The Solemnity of Mary, the Mother of God
Humility is a treasure, because upon the humble the Lord pours every blessing in abundance. [Luke 1:48–53]

2

Humility has been regarded by the saints as the basis and guardian of all virtues....As in the structure of an edifice, the foundation takes precedence of the walls, and even of the golden ornaments.

3

Humility must precede all other virtues.

4

To be angry at ourselves after the commission of a fault is a fault worse than the one [already] committed and will be the occasion of many other faults.

5

It is a delusion of the devil to make us consider it a virtue to be angry with ourselves for committing some fault. Far from it! It is a trick of the enemy to keep us in a state of trouble so we may be unfit for the performance of any good.

6

In short, to remain constantly united with Jesus Christ, we must do all with tranquility and not be troubled at any contradiction that we may encounter.

7

Meekness is especially necessary when we have to correct others.

8

Saint James writes that as God confers His graces with open hands upon the humble, so does He close them against the proud, whom He resists. [Jas 4:6]

9

A heart full of self cannot be replenished with the gifts of God. To receive the divine favors, the soul must be first emptied by the knowledge of its own nothingness.

10

The humble man is always content, because whatever respect is paid to him he deems to be above his merits, and whatever contempt may be offered to him he regards as far short of what is due to his sins.

11

Humility is truth...and therefore the Lord greatly loves the humble, because they love the truth.

12

Whatever good we have or perform belongs to God and comes from His hands. This truth the humble man keeps continually before his eyes; he therefore appropriates to himself only what is evil, deems himself worthy of all sorts of contempt, and cannot bear to hear others attribute to him what he does not deserve.

13

They who are truly humble possess the most perfect knowledge, not only of the divine perfections, but also of their own miseries and sins....The saints, not in the language of exaggeration, but in the sincerity of their souls, called themselves the greatest sinners in the world.

14

Shun, as death itself, every—even the most trifling—act or thought of pride.

15

Humiliation is preferable to all the applause and honor which the world can bestow.

16

He who in passing through a door bends his head more than is necessary is free from all danger of injury, but he who carries it too high may be seriously hurt. Be careful, then, to speak of yourself humbly rather than boastingly.

17

Unless we are like little children, not in years but in humility, we shall never attain salvation.

18

Affronts, poverty, torments, and all tribulations serve only to estrange further from God the soul that does not love Him; whereas, when they befall a soul in love with God, they become an instrument of closer union and more ardent love of [Him].

19

The proud man relies on his own strength and falls on that account; but the humble man, by placing all his trust in God alone, stands firm and falls not.

20

Whoever styles himself the greatest sinner in the world, and then is angry when others despise him, plainly shows that he has humility of tongue, but not of heart.

21

Jesus, by His humility, merited for us the grace of conquering pride.

22

The enemy traffics for Hell when he infects the soul with the desires of esteem [of the world] because, by thus laying aside humility, [the soul] runs great risks of plunging into every vice.

23

The only begotten of God humbled Himself so as to wash the feet of His creatures....He wished to place Himself at the feet of His servants in order to leave us, at the end of His life, this great example of humility and this proof of the great love that He bears to [His people].

24

He that loves God does not desire to be esteemed and loved by his fellow men; the single desire of his heart is to enjoy the favor of Almighty God, who alone forms the object of his love.

25

Of what use is it to pass for great in the eyes of the world, if before God we be vile and worthless? And on the contrary, what does it matter to be despised by the world, provided we be dear and acceptable in the eyes of God?

26

He who loves God is humble and is not elated at seeing any worth in himself; because he knows that whatever he possesses is the gift of God.

27

A single act of humility is worth more than all the riches of the universe.

28

The ambition of a soul that loves God should be to excel all others in humility.

29

The humble, who trust in the Lord, shall renew their strength; distrusting themselves, they shall lay aside their own weakness and put on the strength of God.

30

Let us especially be on our guard against all ambitious seeking of preference and sensibility in points of honor.

31

He who is truly humble never supposes himself humbled as much as he deserves.

February

The Four Last Things
Death, Judgment, Heaven, and Hell

1

The time of death is the time of truth; [only] then do all worldly things appear as they really are: vanity, smoke, and dust.

2

O great secret of death! How it destroys all worldly desires! How it exposes all worldly grandeur as smoke and deceit! Things the most desired of this earth lose all their splendor when beheld from the bed of death.

3

Sooner or later we must die. In every age, houses and cities are filled with new inhabitants and their predecessors consigned to the grave....However long our life may be, an hour will come which will be our last.

4

Would not that traveler be guilty of great folly who should consume all he had in building himself a dwelling in a place which he must soon leave?

5

He who reflects that in a short time he must leave the world will not be attached to it.

6

Hell...[will] at the hour of death put forth all its strength to make us distrust the Divine Mercy, by placing before our eyes all the sins of our life. But the memory of the Death of Jesus Christ will give us courage to trust in His merits and not fear death.

7

Saint Paul writes that Jesus Christ chose to endure death, that through death He might destroy him who had the power of death, that is, the devil. [Heb 2:14]

8

He who dies embracing the Cross has a sure pledge of eternal life, which is promised to all those who follow Jesus Christ with their cross.

9

Let us offer ourselves to God, declaring that we wish to die when it pleases Him, and to accept death in the manner and at the time which He has appointed, ever praying that through the merits of Jesus Christ,...[we will] depart from this life in His grace.

10

We ought not to fear death, but sin, which alone makes death so terrible.

11

Every Christian, in order to live well, ought always to keep eternity before his eyes. Oh how well regulated is the life of that man who lives and sees all things in light of eternity.

12

If Heaven, Hell, and eternity were doubtful things, surely [even then] we ought to do all in our power not to run the risk of being lost forever. But no, they are not doubtful things, but articles of faith.

13

Place yourself, in imagination, in the same situation in which you will be when dying, when not more than an hour will remain for you. Imagine that in a very short time you will have to be presented before your Judge, Jesus Christ, to render an account of your whole life. Nothing will then so much alarm you as remorse of conscience. Put, therefore, [your] accounts in order before the arrival of that great accounting day.

14

There is no medium: either forever a king in Heaven or forever a slave of Lucifer [in Hell]; either forever blessed in Heaven, or forever in despair in Hell.

15

To what will all the fortunes of this world come? To a funeral, to a descent into the grave. Blessed is he who obtains eternal life!

16

What does it matter if we are poor, despised, or sick? If saved, we shall be happy forever. On the contrary, what does it avail to be great or to be monarchs? If lost, we shall be miserable for eternity.

17

God is more desirous of our salvation than the devil is for our perdition.

18

God desires that all should be saved....If we are lost, it will be entirely our own fault.

19

Jesus will come to judge us, appearing with the same wounds that He received for us in His Passion. These wounds will be a source of great consolation to penitents, who with true sorrow have bewailed their sins during life, but will be a source of great terror to sinners who have died in their sins.

20

The greatest torment of the damned will be to reflect that they are lost willfully, through their own fault, despite the fact that Jesus Christ died to save them. "God," they will say, "gave His Life for our salvation, and we fools willfully cast ourselves into this furnace of fire to burn forever!"

21

He who goes to Hell, goes of his own accord. Everyone who is damned, is damned because he wills his own damnation.

22

Those who are lost are not lost for want of means of satisfaction, but because they would not avail themselves of the Sacraments as the means of profiting by the satisfaction made by Jesus Christ.

23

All the damned have been lost through not praying; if they had prayed, they would not have been lost. And this is, and will be, their greatest torment in Hell, to think how easily they might have been saved, only by asking God for His grace; but it is too late—their time of prayer is over.

24

What joy will he experience in hearing it said to him, "Well done, you good and faithful servant; enter into the joy of Thy Lord. Be glad and rejoice, for now you are saved, and there is no longer any fear of being lost." [Matt 25:21]

25

We have a great esteem for the advantages of this life; [then] why do we make so little account of the advantages of eternity?

26

[In Heaven] there are no persecutions; no envy. In that kingdom of love, all love one another tenderly; and each rejoices in the good of the other as if it were his own.

27

[In Heaven, the soul will also] clearly see all the graces which God bestowed upon it [while on earth], in delivering it from so many temptations and so many dangers of perdition; it will then understand that the tribulations, infirmities, persecutions, and losses, which it called misfortunes and divine chastisements, were all love, all means intended by Divine Providence to conduct it to Heaven.

28

In Heaven there is no infirmity, no poverty, no distress; there are no longer the vicissitudes of days and nights, nor of cold and heat; but a perpetual day always serene, an eternal spring always delightful.

29

There are no fears [in Heaven]; because the soul, being confirmed in grace, can no longer sin nor lose its God.

March

The Power of Prayer

1

Prayer obtains every grace that is asked for; it vanquishes all the strength of the tempter; it changes men from blind to [sighted], from weak to strong, from sinners to saints.

2

Let him who wants light, ask it of God and it shall be given.

3

How could we ever observe God's precepts—especially since Adam's sin, which has rendered us so weak and infirm—unless we had prayer as a means whereby we can obtain from God sufficient light and strength to enable us to observe them?

4

Our strongest armor with which we shall win the victory over the assaults of Hell is prayer.

5

By praying, our salvation is made secure and very easy.

6

Trusting in God's promises, let us always pray with confidence....It is perfectly certain that God is faithful in His promises; so ought our faith also be perfectly certain that He will hear us when we pray.

7

From these two premises: on the one hand, that we can do nothing without the assistance of grace, and on the other, that this assistance is only given ordinarily by God to the [person] who prays— who does not see that the consequence follows, that prayer is absolutely necessary for salvation?

8

By prayer we can do all things, for by this means God will give us that strength which we lack.

9

If God were to allow us to present our petitions to Him once a month, even this would be a great favor. The kings of the earth give audiences a few times a year, but God gives a continual audience.

10

By reading and meditating we learn our duty, but by prayer we obtain the grace to do it. What is the use of knowing our duty and then not doing it but to make us more guilty in God's sight?

11

Read and meditate as we like, we shall never satisfy our obligations unless we ask of God the grace to fulfill them.

12

God knows how useful it is to us to be obliged to pray, in order to keep us humble and to exercise our confidence; and He therefore permits us to be assaulted by enemies too mighty to be overcome by our own strength, that by prayer we may obtain from His Mercy the help to resist them.

13

Chastity is a virtue which we have not strength to practice unless God gives it to us; and God does not give this strength except to him who asks for it....Whoever prays for it will certainly obtain it.

14

Wrongly do those sinners excuse themselves who say that they have no strength to resist temptation. We are weak, but God is strong; when we ask Him for help, He communicates His strength to us, and we shall be able to do all things.

15

Our prayers are so dear to God that He has appointed the angels to present them to Him as soon as they come forth from our mouths. [Rev 8:3–4]

16

He is Infinite Majesty, but at the same time He is Infinite Goodness, Infinite Love. He disdains not, but delights that we show toward Him that confidence, that freedom and tenderness, that children show toward their parents.

17

He who prays is certainly saved; he who prays not is certainly damned. All the blessed...have been saved by prayer. All the damned have been lost through not praying; if they had prayed, they would not have been lost.

18

God has promised to give us sufficient help to conquer every temptation, if only we ask Him.

19

Feast of Saint Joseph

The dignity of Saint Joseph is superior to that of all the saints, excepting only that of the Virgin Mother.

20

God gives to all the grace of prayer, in order that thereby they may obtain every help, and even more than they need, for keeping the Divine Law and for persevering until death.

21

If we are not saved, the whole fault will be ours, and we shall have our own failure to answer for, because we did not pray.

22

If you ask me by what means you may conquer temptations I reply: The first means is prayer, the second is prayer, the third is prayer. Were you to ask me a thousand times, I would a thousand times make the same reply.

23

All the saints have become saints by mental prayer....In mental prayer the soul is filled with holy thoughts, desires, and resolutions, and with love for God.

24

What does it cost us to say, "My God, help me! Lord, assist me! Have mercy on me!" Is there anything easier than this? And this little will suffice to save us, if we will be diligent in doing it.

25

God does indeed wish to give us eternal life and therein all graces, but He wishes that we should never omit to ask Him for them, even to the extent of being troublesome.

26

We need not fear the attacks we must endure from the world and from Hell. If we take heed ever to have recourse to Jesus Christ with prayer, He will obtain for us every blessing. He will obtain for us patience in all our labors, perseverance, and in the end will grant us a good death.

27

We should be always crying to God for aid to avoid the death of sin and to advance in His holy love.

28

As moisture is necessary for the life of plants, to prevent them from drying up, so, says Saint John Chrysostom, is prayer necessary for our salvation.

29

Saint Bernard exhorts us to have continual recourse to the Mother of God, because her prayers are certain to be heard by her Son.

30

The devil is never busier to distract us with the thoughts of worldly cares than when he perceives us praying and asking God for grace....And why? Because the enemy sees that at no other time do we gain so many treasures of heavenly goods as when we pray.

31

He who prays, conquers; he who prays not, is conquered.

April

The Holy Sacrifice of the Mass and Reception of Holy Communion

1

The Sacrifice of the Mass, instituted by Our Lord before His Death, is a continuation of the Sacrifice of the Cross.

2

Jesus Christ wished that the price of His Blood, shed for the salvation of [all], should be applied to us by the Sacrifice of the Altar, in which the victim offered is the same, though it is offered differently from how it is on the Cross—that is, without the shedding of blood.

3

Jesus Christ has paid the price of our redemption in the Sacrifice of the Cross, but He wishes that the ransom given should be applied to us in the Sacrifice of the Altar.

4

The Sacrifice of the Altar is really the same Sacrifice as that of the Cross, Jesus Christ being there the principal offerer and the victim that is being offered.

5

The Holy Sacrifice of the Mass is, before all, offered for the Catholic Church by praying to God that He may preserve Her in peace, may defend Her, maintain Her in unity, and govern Her through the ministry of [Her] pastors, by communicating to them His Holy Spirit.

6

We who are travelers upon earth, form only one body with the saints who are in Heaven, and united with them in the same Spirit, we offer to God the same sacrifice.

7

The Sacrifice of Jesus Christ will never cease, since the Son of God will always continue to offer Himself to His Father by an eternal sacrifice, for He Himself is an eternal victim and an eternal priest according to the order of Melchizedek, as David predicted. [Ps 109:4]

8

During the Mass we can obtain all graces that we desire for ourselves and for others.

9

We are unworthy of receiving any grace from God, but Jesus Christ has given us the means of obtaining all graces if, while we offer Him to God in the Mass, we ask [for the graces] of the Eternal Father in His Name, for then Jesus Himself unites with us in prayer.

10

By each Mass more satisfaction is made to God than by any other expiatory work. But although the Mass is of infinite value, God accepts it only in a finite manner, according to the dispositions of those who attend the Holy Sacrifice; therefore it is useful to hear several Masses.

11

The priest, in the prayer which he recites while mixing the water with the wine, beseeches God to grant that, as His Divine Son became partaker of our humanity, we may be made partakers of His Divinity.

12

If at the Mass we make mention of the saints, we do so only because of the graces that they have received from God, to whom they acknowledge they are indebted for all the happiness that they possess.

13

How can a soul be more perfectly united with Jesus than in the manner of which He speaks Himself, saying, "He that eats My flesh and drinks My blood abides in me and I in him" (John 6:57).

14

Saint Denis the Areopagite says that love always tends toward union with the object beloved. And because food becomes one...with him who eats it,...our Lord would reduce Himself to food in order that, receiving Him in Holy Communion, we might become of one substance with Him.

15

In Holy Communion Jesus unites Himself to the soul, and the soul to Jesus; and this is not a union of mere affection, but a true and real union.

16

If there is question of healing our spiritual infirmities, what more certain remedy can we have than… Holy Communion, which is called by the Sacred Council of Trent "a remedy whereby we may be freed from daily faults, and be preserved from mortal sins." [Session 13, Decree on the Most Holy Eucharist, Chapter 2]

17

The saints derived great benefit from their Communions, because they prepared themselves with very great care. Saint Aloysius Gonzaga devoted three days to his preparation for Holy Communion.

18

To prepare better for Holy Communion, a soul should be disposed on two main points: It should be detached from creatures and have a great desire to advance in Divine Love.

19

Since Jesus Christ has so great a desire to come into our souls, it is right that we also should have a great desire to receive Him and His Divine Love by Holy Communion.

20

The Holy Eucharist protects the soul against temptations and it extinguishes the fire of concupiscence.

21

Souls who stay away from Holy Communion because they do not experience in themselves a great degree of sensible devotion resemble, according to the saying of John Gerson, those who feel the cold yet refuse to approach the heat because they do not experience in themselves any sense of warmth!

22

There is no prayer more agreeable to God, or more profitable to the soul, than that which is made during the thanksgiving after Communion.

23

The acts formed in prayer after Communion are far more precious and meritorious in the sight of God than when made at another time; for the soul being then united with Jesus, the value of the acts is increased by [His] presence.

24

Oh, what treasures of grace would you receive, devout soul, if only you entertained yourself with Jesus for an hour, or at least half an hour, after Communion!

25

Holy souls endeavor to remain as long as possible in prayer after Communion.

26

Saint Teresa of Avila says that Jesus, after Communion, remains in the soul as on a throne of grace, and says to it: "What wilt thou that I should do for thee?" (Mark 10:51)

27

Saint Francis de Sales writes that the principal intention of a soul in receiving Communion should be to advance in the love of God. [*Introduction to the Devout Life*, Part 2, Chapter 21]

28

A soul can do nothing that is more pleasing to God than to communicate [that is, receive Holy Communion] in the state of grace.

29

When Jesus comes to the soul in Holy Communion, He brings to it every grace.

30

He who communicates most frequently will be freest from sin and will make the farthest progress in Divine Love.

May

Mary, Our Mother

1

Mary is truly our Mother, not indeed carnally, but spiritually, of our souls and of our salvation.

2

Mary is the Mother who gives birth to holy hope in our hearts, not to the vain and transitory goods of this life, but of the eternal rewards of Heaven.

3

[When] in dangers of sinning, when assailed by temptations, when doubtful as to how you should act, remember that Mary can help you, and if you call upon her, she will instantly help you.

4

No sinner, having recourse to the compassion of Mary, should fear being rejected; for she is the Mother of Mercy, and as such desires to save the most miserable.

5

O Mary, see, I have recourse to thee; in thee do I confide. Thou pray for so many others, pray also for me; say only a word. Tell our Lord that thou will my salvation, and God will certainly save me. Say that I am thine, and then I have obtained all that I ask, all that I desire.

6

In order that we may be preserved in the life of grace, we require spiritual fortitude to resist the many enemies of our salvation. Now this fortitude can be obtained only by the means of Mary, and we are assured of it in the Book of Proverbs, for the Church applies the passage [from Prov 8:15] to this most Blessed Virgin: "Strength is mine; by me kings reign."

7

When a soul loses devotion to Mary, it is immediately enveloped in darkness, and in that darkness of which the Holy Ghost speaks in the Psalms: "Thou hast appointed darkness, and it is night; in it shall all the beasts of the woods go about" (Ps 103:20). When the light of Heaven ceases to shine in a soul, all is darkness, and it becomes the haunt of devils and of every sin.

8

It was not without reason that Saint Germanus called the most Blessed Virgin the breath of Christians; for as the body cannot live without breathing, so the soul cannot live without having recourse to and recommending itself to Mary, by whose means we certainly acquire and preserve the life of divine grace within our souls.

9

Bernardine de Bustis relates that a bird was taught to say, "Hail, Mary!" A hawk was on the point of seizing it, when the bird cried out, "Hail, Mary!" In an instant the hawk fell dead. God intended to show thereby that if even an irrational creature was preserved by calling on Mary, how much more would those who are prompt in calling on her when assaulted by devils, be delivered from them.

10

When tempted by the devil, says Saint Thomas of Villanova, we need only imitate little chickens, which, as soon as they perceive the approach of a bird of prey, run under the wings of their mother for protection. This is exactly what we should do whenever we are assaulted by temptation: We should not stay to reason with it, but immediately fly and place ourselves under the mantle of Mary.

11

Mary's love for her Son immensely surpassed the love of all mothers for their children. She loved Jesus, who was at the same time her Son and her God.

12

The pain which the Holy Virgin endured in the Passion of her Son exceeded all the pains which a human heart can endure.

13

Jesus [while on the Cross] called Mary *woman* to show that she was the great woman foretold in the Book of Genesis who would crush the serpent's head [Gen 3:15]. This woman is the Blessed Virgin Mary, who, by means of her Son, would crush the head of Satan; if it be not more correct to say that her Son, by means of her who would bear Him, would do this.

14

God said to the serpent [in Gen 3:15]: "I will put enmities between your seed and the woman," [which shows] that after the fall of man through sin,…there would be two families…in the world: the seed of Satan, signifying the family of sinners…and the seed of Mary, signifying the Holy Family, which includes all the just, with their Head, Jesus Christ. Hence, Mary was destined to be the Mother both of the Head and of the members [who] are all the spiritual children of Mary.

15

No one denies that Jesus Christ is our only mediator of justice, and that by His merits has obtained our reconciliation with God. But on the other hand, it is impious to assert that God is not pleased to grant graces at the intercession of His saints… especially of Mary His Mother, whom Jesus desires so much to see loved and honored by all.

16

It is impossible for a client of Mary, who is faithful in honoring and recommending himself to her, to be lost....[This] is to be understood of those who, with a sincere desire to amend, are faithful in honoring and recommending themselves to the Mother of God.

17

Mary, by her intercession, obtains for her servants the gifts of Divine Love, holy fear, heavenly light, and holy perseverance.

18

The grace that the Blessed Virgin received exceeded not only that of each particular saint, but of all the angels and saints put together.

19

If [a sinner] recommends himself to this good Mother with perseverance and purpose of amendment, she will undertake to obtain for him light to abandon his wicked state, sorrow for his sins, perseverance in virtue, and, finally, a good death.

20

O, how enraged is the devil when he sees a soul persevering in devotion to the Divine Mother! We read in *The Life of Blessed Alphonsus Rodriguez* [now a canonized saint], who was very devout toward Mary, that once when in prayer, [he found] himself much troubled by the devil with impure thoughts, [and] this enemy said, "Give up thy devotion to Mary, and I will cease to tempt thee."

21

Most Holy and Immaculate Virgin! Thou who art the Mother of my Lord, the Queen of the world, the advocate, hope, and refuge of sinners! I, the most wretched among them, now come to thee. From thee I ask a true love of Jesus Christ, and the grace of a happy death. By thy love for God I beseech thee…[not to leave] me until thou see me safe in Heaven, there for endless ages to bless thee and sing thy praises.

22

All graces are dispensed at Mary's prayer.

23

Where there is no prayer from Mary, there can be no hope of mercy.

24

And now that we have the Son as Mediator with the Eternal Father, and the Mother with the Son, we have full access to God and can go to Him with absolute confidence, hoping for every good thing from Him.

25

Oh, how many blessed souls are now in Heaven who would never have been there had not Mary, by her powerful intercession, led them there!

26

Mary has the will to save us, for she is our Mother and desires our salvation more than we can desire it ourselves.

27

Is there any mother who would not save her child from death, if all she had to do was ask the favor from the judge? And can we imagine that Mary, who loves her [children] with the most tender love a mother ever had, would not save her children from eternal death, when she can do it so easily?

28

In the old cities of refuge, protection was not extended to every class of crime. But under Mary's mantle all sinners without exception find refuge for every sin they have committed, if only they go there to seek this protection.

29

When a soul in sin begins to show signs of devotion to Mary, it is a clear indication that before very long God will enrich it with His grace.

30

The Blessed Virgin herself revealed to Saint Bridget that there is no sinner in the world, however far from God, who does not come back to Him and recover grace, if such a sinner has recourse to her assistance.

31

O Holy Virgin Mary, my Mother and my hope, recommend me to thy Son and obtain for me faithfulness to love Him until my death.

June

Jesus and His Sacred Heart

1

The blood of goats and calves effected merely a carnal purification, while the Blood of Jesus effected the purification of the soul by the remission of sins.

2

All the graces that we obtain are given to us chiefly in view of the merits of Jesus Christ.

3

Who, indeed, at the sight of a crucified God dying for our love can refuse to love Him? Those thorns, those nails, those wounds, and that Blood call upon us and irresistibly urge us to love Him who has loved us so much.

4

What a cause of wonder it must have been to the angels to behold their innocent Lord led as a victim to be sacrificed on the Altar of the Cross for the love of [all]!...Behold, O [people], how far the love of Jesus for us has carried Him, in order to cleanse us from the filthiness of our sins.

5

That which most inflamed Saint Paul with the love of Jesus was the thought that He chose to die not only for all...but for him in particular: "[He] loved me, and delivered Himself up for me" (Gal 2:20).

6

Let us go quickly and embrace the Cross of Jesus Christ, and let us go with great confidence. Let us not be frightened by the sight of our miseries; in Jesus Crucified we shall find all riches, all grace.

7

Alas, how many Christians keep a beautiful crucifix in their room, but only as a fine piece of furniture! They praise the workmanship and the expression of grief, but it makes as little impression on their hearts as if it were, not the image of the Incarnate Word, but [that] of a man who was a stranger and unknown to them.

8

As the waters of the sea are all salt and bitter, so the life of Jesus Christ was full of bitterness and void of all consolations.

9

Moreover, as all the waters of earth unite in the sea, so did all the sufferings of men unite in Jesus Christ.

10

Before the Incarnation of the Word, [we] might have doubted whether God loved [us] with a true love, but after the coming of the Son of God, and after His dying for the love of [all], how can we possibly doubt His love?

11

God recognizes as His own only those who are united with Jesus Christ.

12

The priesthood of Jesus Christ will be eternal, since, even after the end of the world, He will always continue to offer in Heaven this same victim that He once offered on the Cross for the glory of God and for the salvation of mankind.

13

Whatever blessing, whatever salvation, whatever hope we have, we have it all in Jesus Christ and in His merits. [Acts 4:12]

14

There is no hope of salvation for us except through the merits of Jesus Christ.

15

Let us place often before our eyes, especially on Fridays, Jesus dying on the Cross, and let us rest there a while and contemplate the love which He bore to us while He continued in agony upon that bed of pain.

16

How is it that so many Christians, although they know by faith that Jesus Christ died for love of them, instead of devoting themselves wholly to love and serve Him, devote themselves to offend and despise Him for the sake of brief and miserable pleasures? Whence comes this ingratitude? It comes from their forgetfulness of the Passion and Death of Jesus Christ.

17

From the Passion of Jesus Christ all the saints have drawn those flames of love which made them forget the things of this world and even their own selves, to give themselves up wholly to love Jesus Christ.

18

To acquire a true love of Jesus Christ should be our only care.

19

What heart among all hearts can be found more worthy of love than the Heart of Jesus?

20

O Amiable Heart of Jesus, you deserve the love of all hearts; poor and wretched is the heart that loves you not.

21

Oh, if we could only understand the love that burns in the Heart of Jesus for us!

22

Jesus loves us infinitely more than we love ourselves.

23

There never was a moment from eternity that God did not think of us and did not love each one of us. [Jer 31:3]

24

Jesus has loved us more than His honor, more than His comfort, and more than His very life. He sacrificed everything to show us the love that He bears us.

25

By the New Covenant, Jesus Christ, fully satisfying the Divine Justice for the sins of [all], by His merits obtained for [them] pardon and Divine Grace.

26

Jesus has no need of us. He is equally happy, equally rich, equally powerful with or without our love, and yet...He loves us so.

27

My dearest Savior, in Thy merits do I place my hope; oh, do Thou make Thyself to be loved forever...by a sinner who has offended Thee greatly.

28

The principal sorrow which afflicted the Heart of Jesus so much was not the sight of the torments and infamy which men were preparing for Him, but the sight of their ingratitude toward His immense love.

29

Has not Jesus Christ done enough to deserve our love?

30

Where shall we find a heart more compassionate...than the Heart of Jesus?

July

The Theological Virtues of Faith, Hope, and Charity

1

Whoever loves a person, believes all that proceeds from the lips of that person. Consequently, the more a soul loves Jesus Christ, the more lively and unshaken is its faith.

2

Faith is necessary, for had not faith assured us of it, who could ever believe what God has actually done for the love of us?

3

Who, had he not the infallible assurance of faith, could at the sight of Jesus born in a stable believe that He is the God who is adored in Heaven...or that He who was bound to a pillar and suspended on a gibbet is the Lord of the universe?

4

Oh, if [men] would but once forsake sin and apply themselves earnestly to the love of Jesus Christ, they would then most certainly cast away all doubts about things of faith, and firmly believe all the truths that God has revealed!

5

Saint Teresa of Avila says that all our faults and attachments to the goods of this earth arise from a want of faith. Let us then reanimate our faith, [considering] that we shall one day have to leave all and go into eternity.

6

Though God, in order to make our faith more meritorious, has veiled the objects of faith in darkness and secrecy, He has at the same time given us so clear and convincing evidence of their truth, that not to believe them would argue not merely a lack of sense, but sheer madness and impiety.

7

The weakness of faith in many persons is to be traced to their wickedness in living.

8

True confidence in God does not consist in feeling it but in willing it;...if you want to have trust in God then you already have it.

9

Let us be sure of what [Saint Paul] says, that all the sufferings of this life are short and light in comparison with the boundless and eternal joys which we hope to enjoy in Heaven. [2 Cor 4:17]

10

The King of Heaven, being Infinite Goodness, desires in the highest degree to enrich us with His graces. But because confidence is a necessary condition for being heard, and because He wants to increase our confidence, He has given us His own Mother as our Mother and intercessor, and has granted her all power to help us. So it is that He wishes us to place our hope for salvation and every blessing in her.

11

Those who put their trust in Mary, who (being the Mother of God) is able to secure grace and eternal life for them, are truly blessed and acceptable to the Heart of God. Surely He desires to see this greatest of His creatures honored, since she loved and honored Him in this world more than all human beings and angels together.

12

All our hopes are placed in the merits of Jesus Christ....For he who trusts in Jesus Christ is strengthened with an invincible power.

13

What hope for salvation would sinners have were it not for the Cross on which Jesus Christ died to save them?

14

How can I be afraid of not receiving forgiveness, salvation, and every grace from an omnipotent God who has given me all His Blood?

15

How can even the greatest sinner (if he repent of his sins) ever despair of the Divine Mercy at the sight of Jesus Crucified when he knows that the Eternal Father has placed on His Beloved Son all our sins that He might atone for them?

16

When did it ever happen that a man had confidence in the Lord and was lost? [Sir 2:10–11]

17

It is perfectly reasonable to call the Blessed Virgin our hope. We trust...that we shall obtain through her intercession the graces we would not obtain through our own unaided prayers.

18

The first object of our hopes is eternal blessedness, that is, the blessedness of God....All the means which are necessary for obtaining this salvation, we must hope for not from our own strength nor from our good resolutions, but solely from the merits and grace of Jesus Christ.

19

When the crosses of this life afflict us, let us animate ourselves with the hope of Heaven to bear them patiently.

20

Hope increases charity and charity increases hope.

21

The Heart of Jesus is so grateful that it cannot behold the most trifling works done for the love of Him—our smallest word spoken for His glory, a single good thought directed toward pleasing Him—without giving to each its own reward.

22

All good consists in loving God, and loving God consists in doing His will.

23

Charity and truth always go together.

24

The soul that loves God is heedless of what people say of it and aims only at pleasing God.

25

All other virtues, without charity, profit us nothing; but charity brings with it all virtues. [1 Cor 13:1–5]

26

Let it be remembered that perfect charity consists in loving God for Himself....We love God because, on account of His perfections, He deserves to be loved.

27

Oh, how thoroughly does he who loves Jesus Christ understand the force of that saying of the wise man, "Vanity of vanities, and all is vanity" (Eccl 1:2), that all earthly greatness is mere smoke, dirt, and delusion; that the soul's only welfare and happiness consist in loving his Creator and in doing His will.

28

To measure the advance we have made in the ways of God, let us observe what advance we have made in loving Him.

29

Let us be sure that we will never attain to a great love for God, except through Jesus Christ and unless we have a special devotion to His Passion, by which He procured the Divine Grace for us.

30

Cassian says that he who aspires to perfection should aim at great purity of conscience, because from purity of conscience the soul passes to perfect love.

31

Always ask Jesus Christ to give you His holy love. The grace of loving God, says Saint Francis de Sales, is the grace which contains all the other graces, because he who truly loves God will endeavor to avoid anything that might be displeasing to Him, and will study how to please Him in all things. It is therefore necessary above all things to ask of God the grace to love Him.

August

The Will of God

1
Feast of Saint Alphonsus Liguori

It is not necessary to be rich in this world, to gain the esteem of others, to lead a life of ease....It is only necessary to love God and to do His will. For this single end He created us, for this He preserves our life; and thus only can we gain admittance into Heaven.

2

The exercise which is most essential to be practiced by a soul that desires to please God is to conform itself in all things to the Divine Will, and to embrace with peace all things that are contrary to the senses....This is the continual practice of devout souls, and it is the end to be attained by mental prayer.

3

[Those] of the world look on things with many eyes, that is, [they] have several inordinate views in their actions; as for instance, to please others, to become honored, to obtain riches, and, if nothing else, to please themselves....But the saints have [only] a single eye, with which they keep in view, in all that they do, the sole pleasure of God. [Ps 72: 25–26]

4

He that undertakes a thing solely for the glory of God is not troubled at all, though his undertaking may fail of success; for in truth, by working with a pure intention he has already gained his object, which was to please Almighty God.

5

Those who have nothing else in view in their undertakings than the Divine Will, enjoy that holy liberty of spirit which belongs to the children of God....With the same peace, they address themselves to small and great works, to the pleasant and the unpleasant; it is enough for them if they please God.

6

Let us be persuaded that [when] we desire what God desires, we desire what is best for ourselves; for assuredly God only wishes what is best for us.

7

If we were conformed to the Divine Will in every trouble, we would undoubtedly become saints, and be the happiest of [all people].

8

This should form the chief object of our attention: to keep our will in unbroken union with the will of God in every occurrence of life, be it pleasant or unpleasant.

9

Oh, happy the [person] who lives wholly united to the Divine Will! He is neither puffed up by success or depressed by setbacks; for he well knows that all alike comes from the self-same hand of God....He is not anxious to do many things, but to accomplish with perfection what he knows to be acceptable to God.

10

A great servant of God said it [is] better for us in our actions to have the *will* of God, rather than His *glory* as their sole end; for in doing the will of God, we at the same time promote His glory, whereas in proposing to ourselves the glory of God, we frequently deceive ourselves and follow our own will under the pretext of glorifying God.

11

We must be particularly resigned under the pressure of corporal infirmities, and we must embrace them willingly, both in such a manner and in such a time as God wills. Nevertheless, we ought to employ the usual remedies, for this is what the Lord wills also; but if they do us no good, let us unite ourselves to the will of God, and this will do us more good than health.

12

Peace can never be found by one who leads an irregular life, but only by him who lives in union with God and with His Blessed Will.

13

In short, we ought to regard all things that do or will happen to us as proceeding from the hand of God, and everything that we do, we ought to direct to this one end: the fulfillment of His will, and to do it simply because God wills it to be done.

14

Now what is the way to know what God requires of us? There is no surer way than to practice obedience to our superiors and [spiritual] directors.

15

Solemnity of the Assumption of Mary

From the first moment of her Immaculate Conception in the womb of Saint Anne, [Mary] began to love God with all her strength, and continued to do so....All her thoughts, desires, and affections were of and for God alone....O most sweet Lady and our Mother, thou hast already left the earth and reached thy kingdom, where, as Queen, thou art enthroned above all the choirs of angels.

16

God could guide us all by Himself, but to make us humble He wishes that we submit to His ministers and depend on their directions.

17

To eat through obedience is more meritorious in the sight of God than to fast through self-will.

18

The more one unites his will with the Divine Will, the greater will be his love of God.

19

Mortification, meditation, receiving Holy Communion, acts of fraternal charity are all certainly pleasing to God—but only when they are in accordance with His will.

20

The [one] who follows his own will independently of God's, is guilty of a kind of idolatry. Instead of adoring God's will, he, in a certain sense, adores his own.

21

The greatest glory we can give to God is to do His will in everything. Our Redeemer came on earth to glorify His heavenly Father and to teach us by His example how to do the same.

22

Our Lord frequently declared that He had come on earth not to do His own will, but solely that of His Father: "I came down from heaven, not to do my own will, but the will of Him who sent me" (John 6:38).

23

To do God's will—this was the goal upon which the saints constantly fixed their gaze. They were fully persuaded that in this consists the entire perfection of the soul.

24

During our sojourn in this world, we should learn from the saints now in Heaven how to love God. The pure and perfect love of God they enjoy there consists in uniting themselves perfectly to His will.

25

It would be the greatest delight of the seraphs to pile up sand on the seashore or to pull weeds in a garden for all eternity, if they found out such was God's will.

26

A single act of uniformity with the Divine Will suffices to make a saint.

27

Behold, while Saul was persecuting the Church, God enlightened him and converted him. What does Saul do? What does he say? Nothing else but to offer himself to do God's will: "Lord, what wilt thou have me to do?" (Acts 9:6)

28

The essence of perfection is to embrace the will of God in all things, prosperous or adverse. In prosperity, even sinners find it easy to unite themselves to the Divine Will; but it takes saints to unite themselves to God's will when things go wrong and are painful to self-love.

29

It is true, when one offends us unjustly, God does not will his sin, nor does He concur in the sinner's bad will; but God does, in a general way, concur in the material action by which such a one strikes us, robs us, or does us an injury, so that God certainly wills the offense we suffer and it comes to us from His hands.

30

Those who love God are always happy, because their whole happiness is to fulfill, even in adversity, the will of God.

31

He who unites his will to God's experiences a full and lasting joy: full, because he has what he wants;...lasting, because no one can take his joy from him, since no one can prevent what God wills from happening.

September

The Sacrament of Penance and Penance in General

1

Confession cleanses the soul from the stains which it contracts.

2

Confession not only washes away the stains of the soul, but it also gives it strength against relapse.

3

As to the examination of conscience for those that frequent the Sacraments, it is not necessary to distress the head by efforts to find out all the minute circumstances of venial sins. I would rather see such persons careful to discover the causes and roots of their attachments and tepidity.

4

How can a Christian that has been so daring as to sin grievously against the Divine Majesty—and thus has merited Hell, where he should suffer eternal shame—find an excuse before God for concealing a [mortal] sin in Confession, in order to avoid the transient and trifling embarrassment that would arise from confessing it to a priest?

5

How...can you imagine that a confessor, who is bound by his office to show charity to those who come to the tribunal of penance, should treat you with harshness and severity if you confess your sins to him?

6

The most sorrowful, not the longest, confessions are the best.

7

Some are troubled because they do not feel sorrow....You must be persuaded that true sorrow consists not in feeling it, but in wishing for it.

8

All the merit of virtue is in the will.

9

To acquire purity of conscience, many saints confessed their sins every day. Such was the practice of Saint Catherine of Siena, of Saint Bridget,...of Saint Charles Borromeo, of Saint Ignatius of Loyola, and of many others.

10

We ought to represent [each] Confession to ourselves as the last one of our life and dispose ourselves to make it as one would do, who is at the hour of death.

11

Guard against useless discourses at Confession. Of what use is it to relate to the confessor all the occasions of displeasure that you have received from others, or to make many complaints about your infirmities and tribulations?

12

My God, I love Thee above all things. I hope, through the Blood of Jesus Christ, for the pardon of all my sins, for which I am sorry with my whole heart, because by them I have offended and displeased Thy Infinite Goodness. I propose, with Thy grace, never more to offend Thee.

13

My beloved Redeemer, grant that when I first behold Thee [at my judgment], I may see Thee with an appeased countenance; and for this end give me now light, give me strength to reform my life. I desire always to love Thee. If I have despised Thy graces, I now esteem them above all the kingdoms of the world.

14

Reflect that the Most Blessed Trinity—Father, Son, and Holy Spirit, the only and almighty God—is everywhere present; that He sees all things, knows all things, and penetrates the most secret thoughts of our heart.

15

Let us cast ourselves at the feet of the crucifix and turn our attention to the state of our souls, and if we find them unprepared to appear before Jesus Christ, let us correct and amend them now, while we still have the time.

16

As for those who seldom approach the Sacrament [of Penance], it is their duty to employ sufficient time to make a diligent examination of their consciences, and to call to mind as nearly as possible…[how] they have failed in thought, word, or deed.

17

It must be observed by persons of a timorous disposition, who often approach the Sacraments, that their examination ought to be short and unaccompanied with disquietude and scrupulosity. It is sufficient for persons of this description to take a momentary view of the faults into which they are accustomed to fall, and then principally apply themselves to acts of devotion and contrition, which are always the most essential for this Sacrament.

18

For the scrupulous, it is not advisable to confess their doubts.

19

There is no more secure way of countering the temptations of the devil than by obeying the directions of your spiritual director in all that concerns God.

20

When the confessor speaks to you on the direction of your conscience, be careful not to interrupt him, and attend to what he says without thinking of anything else. There are some who are very anxious to speak to their confessor, but when he speaks, they pay very little attention to his admonitions.

21

An obedient soul is the delight of God.

22

Nothing but self-will can separate us from God. Neither all the [people] upon earth nor all the devils in Hell can deprive us of His grace....Let [people] give up their own will, and for them there shall be no Hell.

23

Your progress in virtue will be proportionate to your denial of self-will.

24

From what source arise all our troubles? Do they not arise from attachment to our own inclinations?

25

A great servant of God used to say that to perform a single act of abnegation of self-will is more profitable than to build a thousand hospitals.

26

By suffering patiently what He endured in His Passion, Jesus Christ became the cause of eternal life to all those who obediently suffer with patience the troubles of this present life.

27

The cross of the wicked thief, being endured with impatience, became to him a precipice leading to Hell; while the cross endured with patience by the good thief became to him a ladder to paradise.

28

If denied lawful pleasures, the body will not dare to seek forbidden indulgence; but if continually gratified by every innocent enjoyment, it will soon draw the soul into sinful gratifications.

29

O my Jesus, I have offended Thee, I repent of it with all my heart. From this time on I wish to serve Thee, to obey Thee, and to love Thee.

30

The soul that has been created for no other end than to love God, and to live in union with Him, will never be able to find peace or happiness in sensual enjoyments—God alone can make it perfectly content.

October

Adoration of Jesus in the Most Blessed Sacrament

1

Our Holy Faith teaches us, and we are bound to believe, that in the consecrated Host, Jesus Christ is really present....We must also understand that He is thus present on our altars as on a throne of love and mercy, to dispense graces, and there to show us the love which He bears us, by being pleased to dwell night and day, hidden in the midst of us.

2

It is impossible to find on earth a more precious gem, or a treasure more worthy of all our love, than Jesus in the Most Holy Sacrament.

3

There [in front of the Blessed Sacrament] it was that Saint Francis Xavier found refreshment in the midst of his many labors in India; for he employed his days in toiling for souls, and his nights in the presence of the Blessed Sacrament.

4

Saint Francis of Assisi used to go to communicate all his labors and undertakings to Jesus in the Most Holy Sacrament.

5

Be also assured that Jesus Christ finds means to console a soul that remains with a recollected spirit before the Most Blessed Sacrament, far beyond what the world can do with all its feasts and pastimes.

6

Do not think that Jesus Christ is forgetful of you, since He has left you, as the greatest memorial and pledge of His love, Himself in the Most Holy Sacrament of the Altar.

7

All those who desire to advance in the love of Jesus Christ are exhorted to make a spiritual Communion at least once in every visit that they pay to the Most Blessed Sacrament.

8

Let each one of us say in the presence of Jesus in the Blessed Sacrament: "Behold my love! Behold the object of all my love for my whole life and for all eternity!"

9

"My eyes and my heart shall be there always" (1 Kgs 9:3). Behold, Jesus has verified this beautiful promise in the Sacrament of the Altar, wherein He dwells with us night and day.

10

Loving souls can find no greater delight than to be in the company of those whom they love....Let us console ourselves in His company; let us rejoice in His glory....Let us desire that all should love Jesus in the Holy Sacrament, and consecrate their hearts to Him; at least let us consecrate all our affections to Him.

11

It is sweet to everyone to be in the company of a dear friend; and shall we not find it sweet, in this valley of tears, to remain in the company of the best friend we have, and who can do us every kind of good, who loves us with the most tender affection, and therefore dwells always with us?

12

Many Christians submit to great fatigue and expose themselves to many dangers, to visit the places in the Holy Land where our most loving Savior was born, suffered, and died. We need not undertake so long a journey, or expose ourselves to so many dangers; the same Lord is near us and dwells in the church, only a few steps from our houses.

13

Our lost, loving Redeemer instituted the Most Holy Sacrament of the Eucharist, in which He left us His whole self.

14

Jesus would not be separated from us by His Death. He instituted this Sacrament of Love in order to be with us even to the end of the world.

15

Saint Teresa of Avila said that in this world it is impossible for all subjects to speak to the king. But to speak to the King of Heaven...everyone that wishes can find [Him] in the Most Blessed Sacrament.

16

Oh, how Jesus seems continually to exclaim from the altar: "Come to me, all you that labor and are burdened, and I will refresh you" (Matt 11:28).

17

Behold the source of every good: Jesus in the Most Blessed Sacrament.

18

Oh what torrents of grace have the saints drawn from the fountain of the Most Blessed Sacrament!

19

If we were to sacrifice ourselves every moment unto death, we would certainly not recompense in the smallest degree the love that Jesus Christ has shown us in the Most Holy Sacrament.

20

O hidden God, unknown to the greater part of men...I adore Thee in the Most Holy Sacrament as my Lord and Savior!

21

O God, O Infinite Amiability, only worthy object of all my love, I love Thee with my whole heart; I love Thee above all things; I love Thee more than myself.

22

How agreeable those souls are to the Heart of Jesus, who frequently visit Him and remain in His company in the churches in which He is, under the sacramental species.

23

Certainly among all devotions, after receiving the Sacraments, that of adoring Jesus in the Blessed Sacrament holds the first place, is the most pleasing to God, and [is] the most useful to ourselves.

24

Be assured that the time you spend with devotion before this Most Divine Sacrament will be the most profitable to you in life, and the source of your greatest consolation in death and in eternity.

25

Jesus Christ has concealed His Majesty in the Sacrament in order to give us more confidence and to take away from us all fear of approaching Him.

26

Oh, how sweet a joy it is to remain with a recollected spirit before the Most Blessed Sacrament and converse familiarly with Jesus Christ, who is there for the express purpose of listening to and graciously hearing those who pray to Him.

27

The souls that love Jesus Christ much do not know how to wish for any other heaven on this earth than to be in the presence of their Lord, who dwells in this Sacrament for the love of those who seek and visit Him.

28

Hidden in this Sacrament, Thou, for the love of me, remain always on this altar. I, for the love of Thee, will always remain in Thy presence as much as I shall be able.

29

The marks of affection which we receive from our friends at the time of their death remain more deeply impressed on our hearts; for this reason Jesus bestowed on us this gift of the Blessed Sacrament just before His Death.

30

O my most beloved Jesus, what has it cost Thee to remain with us in this Sacrament!

31

The desire of Jesus Christ [is] to console everyone who has recourse to Him, [so] He remains day and night on our altars that He may be found by all and that He may bestow graces upon all.

November

Sin and Suffering

1
The Solemnity of All Saints
The only way by which we can become saints is the way of suffering.

2
Adam sinned and rebelled against God, and being the first man and the progenitor of all,... he fell into a state of perdition, together with the whole human race. The injury was done to God, so that neither Adam nor all the rest of mankind by all the sacrifices that they could have offered, even of their own [lives], could furnish a worthy satisfaction to the Divine Majesty which was offended.

3

There was need that a Divine Person should satisfy the Divine Justice. Behold then, the Son of God who, moved to compassion,...offered Himself to take human flesh and to die for [all people] that He might thus give to God a complete satisfaction for all their sins and obtain for them the Divine Grace which they had lost.

4

Sin had rendered all [of us] unworthy of being offered to God and of being accepted by Him, and therefore, it was necessary that Jesus Christ should offer Himself for us in order to sanctify us by His grace, and to make us worthy of being accepted by God.

5

We are so miserable and our mind is so limited, that we do not even know what graces we should ask of God in behalf of our own salvation. [Rom 8:26]

6

The only evil that we ought to fear is sin.

7

No one is damned for the original sin of Adam, but solely for his own fault, because God [gives to everyone] the grace of prayer, whereby we may obtain His assistance to overcome every temptation.

8

It must be that [mortal] sin is a great evil, since God who is Mercy Itself is obliged to punish it with an eternal Hell. In order to satisfy Divine Justice for sin, God was obliged to sacrifice His own life.

9

The lives of [all people] would not have been sufficient to make satisfaction for a single sin, but the pains of Jesus Christ have paid for all our sins.

10

We have far greater reason to hope for everlasting life through the merits of Jesus Christ, which are infinitely more powerful for our salvation than our sins are for our damnation.

11

We have sinned and have deserved Hell, but the Redeemer came to take upon Himself all our offenses and to make satisfaction for them by His sufferings. [Isa 53:4–5]

12

The proud man trusts in his own courage and therefore yields to temptation.

13

What does he gain who refuses [his own] cross? He increases its weight.

14

Contradictions, sickness, scruples, spiritual aridity, and all the inner and outward torments are the chisel with which God carves His statues for Heaven.

15

All those temptations to blasphemy, unbelief, impurity, and despair are not sins but sufferings, which, if patiently borne, bring the soul nearer and nearer to God.

16

We must rest assured that none will rejoice with Jesus Christ but they who are willing to suffer in this world with Him; nor will he obtain the crown who does not fight as he ought to fight.

17

This earth is the place for meriting, and therefore it is a place for suffering....All must suffer, be they just or be they sinners; each one must carry his cross. He that carries it with patience is saved.

18

Let us who boast that we are disciples of Jesus Christ be ashamed of angrily resenting the injuries which we receive from men, because God-made-man suffered the same for our salvation with so much patience.

19

In the same manner as God has treated His beloved Son, so does He treat everyone whom He loves, and whom He receives for His Son: "For whom the Lord loves He chastises, and He scourges every son whom He receives" (Heb 12:6).

20

Even with regard to the present life, it is certain that he who suffers with the most patience enjoys the greatest peace. It was a saying of Saint Philip Neri that in this world there is no Purgatory; it is either all Heaven or all Hell: he that patiently bears tribulations enjoys a heaven; he that does not do so, suffers a hell.

21

Let us be convinced that, in this valley of tears, true peace of heart cannot be found, except by him who endures and lovingly embraces sufferings to please Almighty God; this is the consequence of that corruption in which all are placed through the infection of sin.

22

The condition of the saints on earth is to suffer and to love; the condition of the saints in Heaven is to enjoy and to love.

23

Oh, what abundance of merits may be accumulated by patiently enduring illnesses! It is by the patient endurance of ill health that we weave a great part...of our crown in Heaven.

24

That we may be able to practice patience to advantage in all our tribulations, we must be fully persuaded that every trial comes from the hands of God either directly, or indirectly through men; we must therefore render God thanks whenever we are beset with sorrows and accept, with gladness of heart,...every event, prosperous or adverse, that proceeds from Him, knowing that all happens by His disposition for our welfare. [Rom 8:28]

25

God has no desire to see us suffer, but being Himself Infinite Justice, He cannot leave our faults unpunished; so in order that they may be punished and yet we may one day attain eternal happiness, He would have us purge away our sins with patience and thus deserve to be eternally blessed. What can be more beautiful and sweet than this rule of Divine Providence, that we see at once justice satisfied and ourselves saved and happy?

26

The merit of a soul that loves Jesus Christ consists in loving and in suffering.

27

When we see ourselves afflicted with the troubles of this life, let us lift up our eyes to Heaven.

28

Let us reflect that if we be faithful to God, all these sorrows, miseries, and fears will one day have an end, and we shall be admitted into that blessed country, where we shall enjoy complete happiness as long as God will be God.

29

When the soul has once entered into the happy kingdom of God, "God shall wipe away all tears from their eyes; and death shall be no more, nor mourning, nor crying, nor sorrow shall be anymore; for the former things are passed away. And He that sat on the throne said: 'Behold I make all things new'" (Rev 21:4).

30

Jesus Christ could easily have obtained for us salvation without suffering and in leading a life of ease and delight, but no; Saint Paul says that, "having joy set before Him, [Christ] endured the cross" (Heb 12:2). He refused the riches, the delights, the honors of the world and chose for Himself a life of poverty and a death full of suffering and ignominy.

December

The Incarnation of Jesus Christ

1

If Jesus Christ had come into the world immediately after the fall of Adam, the greatness of this favor would [still] have been only slightly appreciated.

2

Before the coming of the Messiah, who loved God upon earth? Hardly was He known in a nook of the world, that is, Judea; and even there how very few loved Him when He came!

3

Consider that the Eternal Father, in giving us His Son for a Redeemer...could not have given us stronger motives for hope and love, to inspire us with confidence and to oblige us to love Him.

4

God came from Heaven to arrest, as it were, ungrateful man in his flight from Him. It is as if He had said, "O man! Behold, it is nothing but the love of thee that has brought me on earth to seek after thee....Stay with me....Do not avoid me, for I greatly love thee."

5

It was an immeasurably greater humiliation for God to become man than if all the princes of the earth, than if all the angels and saints of Heaven, had been turned into a blade of grass or into a handful of clay. For grass, clay, princes, angels, saints are all creatures; but between the creature and God there is an infinite difference.

6

O God! If faith did not assure us of it, who could ever believe that God, for love of such a worm as man is, should Himself become a worm like him?

7

God, then, having so dearly loved us, seeks nothing else from us...but our love.

8

Solemnity of the Immaculate Conception of Mary in Her Mother's Womb

Because she was appointed Mediatrix of the world, as also because she was destined to be the Mother of the Redeemer, [Mary] received, at the very beginning of her existence, grace exceeding in greatness that of all the saints together. Hence, how delightful a sight must the beautiful soul of this happy child have been to Heaven and earth, although still enclosed in her mother's womb!

9

The Jews—although by so many signs and wonders had a certain knowledge of the true God—were not satisfied; they wished to behold Him face to face. God found means to comply even with this desire of men; He became man, to make Himself visible to them.

10

To comprehend the idea of the immense love of God [for all] in becoming Himself a feeble child for our love, it would be necessary to comprehend His greatness. But what mind...can conceive the greatness of God, which is indeed infinite?

11

Saint Ambrose says that to say God is greater than the heavens—than all kings, all saints, all angels—is to do an injury to God; just as it would be an injury to a prince to say that he was greater than a blade of grass or a small fly. God is Greatness Itself, and all greatness together is but the smallest atom of the greatness of God.

12

It is a custom with many Christians to anticipate the arrival of Christmas a considerable time beforehand by setting up in their homes a crib to represent the birth of Jesus Christ; but there are few who think of preparing their hearts in order that the Infant Jesus may be born in them, and there find His repose.

13

The angel [Gabriel] salutes Mary, calls her full of grace and blessed among women. He then tells her that her Son is the very Son of God who is to redeem the world and thus reign over the hearts of men. [Luke 1:26–33]

14

Saint Sophronius, Patriarch of Jerusalem, asserts that the reason for which the Archangel Gabriel called [Mary] full of grace was because only limited grace was given to others, but it was given to Mary in all its plenitude.

15

This Son has given more glory and honor to God in the first moment of His [Incarnation] than all the angels and saints together have given Him, or shall give Him for all eternity.

16

Let us thank this Son and let us also thank His Mother, who, in consenting to be the Mother of such a Son, consented also to be the Mother of our salvation.

17

Jesus Christ revealed to Venerable Agatha of the Cross that while He was in His Mother's womb, that which afflicted Him more than any other sorrow was the hardness of the hearts of [those] who would, after His Redemption, despise the graces which He came into the world to dispense.

18

The Son of God became weak and assumed to Himself the bodily infirmities of [humanity], in order to procure for [humanity], by His merits, the strength of soul necessary to subdue the attacks of the flesh.

19

God had decreed that His Son should be born not in the house of Joseph, but in a cavern and stable of beasts, in the poorest way a child can be born.

20

[Mary] knew by divine inspiration, and also because she was well versed in the prophecy of Micah [Mic 5:1–2], that the Divine Infant was to be born in Bethlehem.

21

Let us beseech Jesus, Mary, and Joseph that, through the merits of the pains which they suffered in this journey [from Nazareth to Bethlehem], they would accompany us in the journey that we are making to eternity.

22

Oh, blessed shall we be if, in life and in death, we keep company with these three great personages [of Jesus, Mary, and Joseph] and are always accompanied by them!

23

[Behold] Immensity…whom the heavens cannot contain; see Him imprisoned in poor rags and put in a foul manger on a bundle of straw.

24

Now this God, so great, has become a little infant; and for whom? For us He is born.

25

Solemnity of the Nativity of Our Lord

In order to exempt us from every feeling of distrust, which the idea of His power and of His justice might cause in us, He comes before us as a little baby, full of sweetness and mercy.

26

Little children of themselves are loved at once; to see them and to love them are the same thing. With this view, says Saint Francis de Sales, the Eternal Word chose first to be seen among [us] as an infant, to reconcile to Himself the love of all.

27

The just [person] enjoys unruffled peace. This is the peace promised by the angel of the Nativity: "And on earth, peace to men of good will" (Luke 2:14). Who are these "men of good will" if not those whose wills are united to the infinitely good and perfect Will of God?

28

There is no peace to be found without God.

29

Behold the wise men who immediately set off on their journey. The Infant looks upon them with a joyful expression. See how, out of reverence, they adore Him in silence and acknowledge Him for their God.

30

Let us also with the holy magi adore our little King Jesus, and let us offer Him all our hearts.

31

Jesus appeared as an infant, poor and humble, and showed Himself on earth born in a stable, covered with rags and lying on straw; but at His Second Coming He will come on a throne of majesty [Matt 24:30]. Blessed then will he be who shall have loved Him, and miserable those who have not loved Him.

Bibliography

Liguori, St. Alphonsus. *The Passion and Death of Jesus Christ*. Brooklyn: Redemptorist Fathers, 1927.

Liguori, St. Alphonsus. *The Holy Eucharist*. Brooklyn: Redemptorist Fathers, 1934.

Liguori, St. Alphonsus. *The Great Means of Salvation and of Perfection*. Brooklyn: Redemptorist Fathers, 1927.

Liguori, St. Alphonsus. *The Incarnation, Birth and Infancy of Jesus Christ*. Brooklyn: Redemptorist Fathers, 1927.

Liguori, St. Alphonsus. *The True Spouse of Jesus Christ (The Nun Sanctified)*. Brooklyn: Redemptorist Fathers, 1929.

Liguori, St. Alphonsus. *The Glories of Mary*. Brooklyn: Redemptorist Fathers, 1931.